ETHICS AND VALUE BASED EDUCATION

REIMAGINING JAPAN'S SCHOOL SYSTEM

DR. MINAKSHI BANSAL

Made with ❤ on the Notion Press Platform
www.notionpress.com

DEDICATION

To the next generation of learners, leaders, and changemakers, may you embrace the power of ethical education to shape a brighter future for yourselves and for the world.

❥❥❥

Contents

Contents

Prayer

"Om Bhadram Karnebhih Shrinuyama Devah

Bhadram Pashyemakshabhiryajatrah

Sthirairangais Tushtuvamsastanubhih

Vyashema Devahitam Yadayuh

Svasti Na Indro Vriddhashravah

Svasti Nah Pusha Vishwavedah

Svasti Nastarkshyo Arishtanemih

Svasti No Brihaspatir Dadhatu

Om Shantih Shantih Shantih"

This mantra is a prayer for universal well-being, invoking the blessings of various deities for protection, health, and happiness. It emphasizes the importance of experiencing the auspicious through all senses and living a life aligned with divine purpose. The repetition of "Shantih" at the end signifies a deep desire for peace in the individual, the environment, and the universe at large. This mantra is often recited as a prayer for peace, prosperity, and the physical and spiritual well-being of all beings.

ॐ ॐ ॐ

About The Author

This book represents the culmination of extensive research and meticulous analysis, incorporating a diverse range of sources, including numerous books, scholarly studies, and personal experiences. Additionally, I have scoured various websites to gather relevant information and data essential for the compilation of this work. I have taken every precaution to ensure the accuracy of the information presented and have diligently cited all sources to acknowledge their contributions.

From her earliest days, Minakshi was distinguished by an insatiable appetite for reading. Her literary universe was inhabited by characters and narratives that spanned ethical tales, motivational and inspirational stories, and the mythic parables imbued with life lessons. This voracious reading habit was not merely for personal edification but was driven by a desire to distill and disseminate the essence of these narratives to foster the development of students and peers alike. She was particularly captivated by the lives and teachings of historical figures and spiritual leaders such as Adi Shankaracharya, Swami Vivekananda, Dr. APJ Abdul Kalam, Mahamana Pandit Madan Mohan Malviya, Mahatma Gandhi, Sardar Vallabhai Patel, and Vinoba Bhave, among others. Their philosophies and life stories fueled her ambition to embody their ideals of resilience, selflessness, and relentless pursuit of knowledge.

Dr. Minakshi's academic and practical engagement with psychology has been equally noteworthy. As a research scholar, her focus has been on exploring the intricate tapestry of the human psyche, aiming to unlock the potential for psychological well-being and societal harmony. Her scholarly work is complemented by her active involvement in social work, where she employs her academic insights to make tangible differences in the lives of the underprivileged. Her endeavours in social work are characterized by an innovative approach that combines traditional wisdom with contemporary psychological practices to address the multifaceted challenges faced by these communities.

Her artistic talents, another facet of her diverse capabilities, are not merely a personal passion but also serve as a medium through which she communicates and connects with others. Her art, rich in symbolism and emotional depth, reflects her philosophical inquiries and social concerns, offering viewers a glimpse into the breadth of her intellect and the depth of her compassion.

In addition to her contributions to the arts and social sciences, Dr. Minakshi has embraced the healing arts of Pranic Healing, mastering the techniques developed by Master Choa Kok Sui. This practice, which focuses on the manipulation of Prana or life energy to heal the body and aura, has been both a personal journey of discovery and a means through which she extends her healing touch to others. Her proficiency in Pranic Healing is complemented by her advocacy and teaching of various forms of meditation aimed at rejuvenation, personal betterment, and the cultivation of harmony within individuals and communities alike.

Dr. Minakshi's life is a narrative of relentless pursuit, not just of personal achievement but of the upliftment and empowerment of society at large. Her diverse interests and talents—spanning the arts, literature, psychology, and the healing practices—converge on a singular path of service. She embodies the spirit of the luminaries who inspired her, channelling their legacy through her actions and teachings. Through her books, art, and social initiatives, she continues to inspire a new generation to embark on their own journeys of self-discovery, resilience, and altruism.

Her commitment to social betterment, particularly her focus on uplifting underprivileged children, reflects a deep understanding of the transformative potential of education and personal development. By integrating her knowledge of psychology, her artistic sensibilities, and her healing practices, Dr. Bansal has developed a holistic approach to social work that addresses both the immediate needs and the long-term well-being of the communities she serves.

As an author, Dr. Minakshi's writings offer a blend of inspirational insights, practical wisdom, and reflective contemplations drawn from her extensive reading and life experiences. Her books serve as a guide for those seeking to navigate the complexities of life with grace, resilience, and purpose. Through her narratives, she extends an invitation to her readers to explore the depths of their own potential and to contribute meaningfully to the collective well-being of society.

In Dr. Minakshi Bansal, we find a remarkable synthesis of the artist, the scholar, the healer, and the social activist. Her life's work stands as a beacon of hope and a source of inspiration for individuals seeking to make a difference in the world. Her story is a compelling reminder of the power of individual action, rooted in compassion and driven by a profound commitment to the betterment of humanity. Dr. Minakshi's legacy is not just in the tangible outcomes of her efforts but in the enduring spirit of inquiry, empathy, and service that she embodies.

ᐳᐳᐳ

Preface

The path that led me to write this book, "Ethics and Value Based Education," was paved with a profound sense of urgency and hope. As an educator and researcher deeply invested in the future of Japan's youth, I have witnessed firsthand the transformative power of education. Yet, I have also observed a growing disconnect between academic achievement and the cultivation of ethical values and character.

The relentless pursuit of academic excellence, while undoubtedly important, has often overshadowed the development of essential qualities such as empathy, compassion, critical thinking, and social responsibility. We have created a system that measures success primarily through test scores and university admissions, neglecting the holistic development of our children. This narrow focus on academics not only leaves students ill-equipped to navigate the complexities of the modern world but also perpetuates social inequalities and hinders the creation of a truly harmonious society.

In recent years, Japan has faced a myriad of challenges, from economic stagnation and demographic shifts to environmental concerns and social fragmentation. These challenges demand a new generation of leaders who are not only knowledgeable and skilled but also ethically grounded and committed to the well-being of their communities and the planet. It is my firm belief that education holds the key to cultivating such leaders.

This book is a culmination of years of research, reflection, and dialogue with educators, students, parents, and policymakers. It is a call to action, urging us to reimagine Japan's school system and to prioritize the development pref ethical values alongside academic pursuits. It is a blueprint for creating schools that not only impart knowledge but also nurture character, inspire compassion, and empower students to make a positive difference in the world.

Throughout this book, I explore various facets of ethical and value-based education. I delve into the importance of fostering a supportive and inclusive learning environment where students feel safe to express their opinions and to explore their values. I discuss the need to integrate ethical discussions and dilemmas into the curriculum, providing students with opportunities to grapple with complex issues and to develop their own moral compass. I highlight the importance of experiential learning, where students can apply their knowledge and skills in real-world contexts and develop a sense of social responsibility.

I also examine the role of teachers as mentors and role models, guiding students on their ethical journey. I explore the importance of parental involvement in supporting values education at home and in the community. I emphasize the need for schools to connect with their communities, providing students with opportunities to engage with diverse perspectives and to contribute to the well-being of their society.

Furthermore, I address the importance of global citizenship in an interconnected world, highlighting the ethical implications of technology and the need for environmental responsibility. I discuss the value of diversity and inclusion, emphasizing the importance of valuing all voices and creating a more equitable and just society. I delve into the concept of social justice, empowering students to become agents of change and to challenge systemic inequalities.

Finally, I present a vision for the future, envisioning ethical schools as vibrant communities that nurture values, character, and social responsibility. I offer practical recommendations for how we can transform our schools into places where students not only learn but also grow as ethical individuals and compassionate citizens.

My hope is that this book will spark a national conversation about the importance of ethical and value-based education in Japan. It is my aspiration that it will inspire educators, policymakers, parents, and students to work together to create a more just, equitable, and sustainable future for all. I believe that by reimagining our school system and prioritizing ethical education, we can empower the next generation to become the leaders and changemakers our world so desperately needs.

The journey towards ethical schools will not be easy. It will require a fundamental shift in our mindset, a willingness to challenge traditional norms, and a commitment to collaboration and innovation. However, I am confident that by working together, we can create a brighter future for our children and for our country. The time for change is now. Let us embrace the challenge and create a legacy of ethical education that will inspire generations to come.

Dr. Minakshi Bansal
Social Activist
Ahmedabad, Gujarat, Bharat

ONE

BEYOND ACADEMICS: THE HEART OF ETHICAL EDUCATION

Education has long been hailed as a cornerstone of societal progress, a means of cultivating minds and preparing future generations for the challenges and opportunities that lie ahead. However, a growing consensus recognizes that education must extend beyond mere academic achievement and encompass the development of ethical values and principles. In the context of Japan's education system, renowned for its rigor and emphasis on academic excellence, a paradigm shift is underway towards integrating ethics and values into the core curriculum. This chapter delves into the essence of ethical education, exploring its significance, components, and potential impact on shaping well-rounded individuals and a harmonious society.

At its core, ethical education transcends the acquisition of knowledge and skills. It aims to foster moral reasoning, empathy, and a sense of responsibility towards oneself and others. While academic subjects impart knowledge about the world, ethical education instills the wisdom to navigate complex ethical dilemmas and make choices aligned with one's values. In a rapidly changing and interconnected world, ethical considerations are paramount. Issues such as climate change, social inequality, technological advancements, and globalization demand individuals who can think critically, act responsibly, and contribute to the common good. Ethical education equips students with the tools to address these challenges, fostering a sense of global citizenship and a commitment to ethical decision-making.

The Japanese education system has traditionally emphasized academic rigor and discipline, fostering a competitive environment that often prioritizes test scores and university admissions. However, recent years have witnessed a growing recognition of the need to nurture ethical values alongside academic pursuits. The Ministry of Education, Culture, Sports, Science, and Technology (MEXT) has introduced various initiatives to promote moral education, emphasizing character development, social responsibility, and respect for others. The concept of "ikikata," which translates to "way of living," is central to this approach. It encourages students to reflect on their values, purpose in life, and contribution to society.

Integrating ethical education into the school curriculum requires a multi-faceted approach. First and foremost, it involves creating a supportive and inclusive learning environment that encourages open dialogue and respect for diverse perspectives. Teachers play a crucial role in modeling ethical behavior and facilitating discussions on ethical dilemmas. They can incorporate real-world examples, case studies, and literature to spark critical thinking and promote empathy. Moreover, ethical education should not be confined to specific subjects or lessons. It should permeate the entire school experience, from classroom interactions to extracurricular activities. Schools can establish student councils, volunteer programs, and community engagement initiatives that provide opportunities for students to practice ethical decision-making and social responsibility.

One of the key challenges in implementing ethical education is defining and agreeing upon a set of core values. Japan, with its rich cultural heritage and philosophical traditions, offers a wealth of resources to draw upon. Concepts such as honesty, compassion, respect for elders, and harmony with nature are deeply ingrained in Japanese culture. However, it is important to acknowledge the diversity of values within society and to foster an inclusive approach that respects individual differences while promoting a shared understanding of ethical principles.

The benefits of ethical education extend far beyond the classroom walls. Students who have been exposed to ethical education are more likely to exhibit prosocial behavior, engage in civic activities, and make ethical choices in their personal and professional lives. They are better equipped to navigate complex moral dilemmas, resolve conflicts peacefully, and contribute to a more just and equitable society. Moreover, ethical education can have a positive impact on students' mental and emotional well-being. By cultivating self-awareness, empathy, and a sense of purpose, it can reduce stress, anxiety, and depression, fostering resilience and overall life satisfaction.

In conclusion, the integration of ethics and values into education is essential for the holistic development of individuals and the creation of a harmonious society. By moving beyond academics and emphasizing character development, moral reasoning, and social responsibility, ethical education equips students with the tools to navigate the complexities of the modern world and make ethical choices that benefit themselves, their communities, and the planet. In the context of Japan, with its rich cultural heritage and emphasis on academic excellence, the integration of ethical education represents a promising avenue for fostering well-rounded individuals who are not only knowledgeable but also compassionate, responsible, and committed to creating a better future for all.

ÞÞÞ

Education is not just about filling minds; it's about igniting hearts. Let us empower students to embrace ethical values and become compassionate leaders who shape a brighter future. Remember, true knowledge is not just about knowing; it's about doing what is right.

TWO

VALUES IN THE CLASSROOM: MORE THAN JUST WORDS

The classroom is not merely a space for academic instruction; it is a microcosm of society, a place where young minds are molded and values are instilled. Values, the guiding principles that shape our beliefs, attitudes, and behaviors, are fundamental to the development of well-rounded individuals and a harmonious society. In the context of education, values transcend mere words on a blackboard; they are the invisible threads that weave together the fabric of a meaningful learning experience.

Values education is not a new concept, but its significance has gained renewed prominence in recent years. In an increasingly complex and interconnected world, where ethical dilemmas abound and societal challenges demand innovative solutions, the cultivation of values has become imperative. Values such as honesty, respect, responsibility, compassion, and fairness provide a moral compass that guides individuals in making sound decisions, building healthy relationships, and contributing to the betterment of society.

Within the classroom, values education can take many forms. It can be integrated into the curriculum through discussions, role-playing activities, case studies, and literature. Teachers can model ethical behavior and encourage students to reflect on their own values and beliefs. They can create a safe and inclusive environment where diverse perspectives are respected and students feel empowered to express their opinions.

Values education is not limited to moral instruction. It encompasses a wide range of principles that contribute to personal growth, social cohesion, and environmental sustainability. For example, fostering a sense of curiosity and a love of learning can instill a lifelong passion for knowledge and self-improvement. Promoting teamwork and collaboration can teach students the importance of cooperation and shared responsibility. Encouraging creativity and critical thinking can empower students to challenge assumptions, explore new ideas, and find innovative solutions to problems.

In Japan, values education has a long-standing tradition. The concept of "tokubetsu katsudo," or special activities, emphasizes the development of character and social skills alongside academic achievement. These activities, which include sports, clubs, and volunteer work, provide students with opportunities to practice teamwork, leadership, and community engagement. The Japanese education system also places a strong emphasis on moral education, with subjects such as "dotoku" (ethics) and "shakai" (social studies) exploring ethical dilemmas and promoting social responsibility.

However, values education in Japan faces challenges. The emphasis on academic achievement and conformity can sometimes stifle individuality and critical thinking. The pressure to succeed in entrance exams can lead to stress and anxiety, hindering the holistic development of students. Moreover, the traditional values that have long shaped Japanese society are being challenged by globalization and technological advancements.

To address these challenges, Japanese educators are exploring new approaches to values education. Some schools are adopting more experiential learning methods, such as project-based learning and service learning, which allow students to apply their knowledge and skills in real-world contexts. Others are integrating technology into the classroom, using online resources and social media to connect students with diverse perspectives and global issues.

The benefits of values education are manifold. Students who have been exposed to values education are more likely to exhibit prosocial behavior, engage in civic activities, and make ethical choices in their personal and professional lives. They are better equipped to navigate complex moral dilemmas, resolve conflicts peacefully, and contribute to a more just and equitable society. Moreover, values education can have a positive impact on students' mental and emotional well-being. By cultivating self-awareness, empathy, and a sense of purpose, it can reduce stress, anxiety, and depression, fostering resilience and overall life satisfaction.

In conclusion, values in the classroom are more than just words; they are the building blocks of character, the foundation of a fulfilling life, and the key to a harmonious society. By integrating values education into the curriculum, fostering a supportive and inclusive learning environment, and modeling ethical behavior, educators can empower students to become responsible, compassionate, and engaged citizens who are committed to making a positive difference in the world. As Japan navigates the challenges and opportunities of the 21st century, values education will play a crucial role in shaping the next generation of leaders, innovators, and changemakers.

ppp

The classroom is not merely a space for learning facts; it's a crucible for character development. By fostering collaboration and valuing all voices, we can nurture a generation of empathetic and socially responsible citizens. This starts with recognizing that every student has a unique perspective and a valuable contribution to make.

THREE

A New Curriculum: Teaching Character Alongside Knowledge

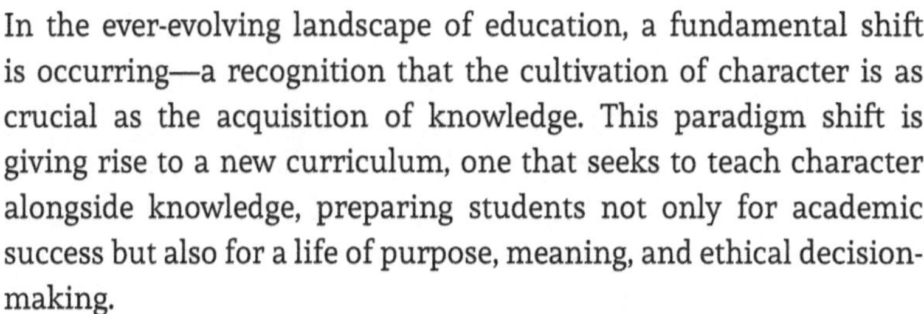

In the ever-evolving landscape of education, a fundamental shift is occurring—a recognition that the cultivation of character is as crucial as the acquisition of knowledge. This paradigm shift is giving rise to a new curriculum, one that seeks to teach character alongside knowledge, preparing students not only for academic success but also for a life of purpose, meaning, and ethical decision-making.

The traditional model of education, with its emphasis on rote memorization, standardized testing, and narrow definitions of success, has often neglected the development of character traits such as empathy, resilience, integrity, and social responsibility. However, in a world grappling with complex challenges such as climate change, social inequality, and political polarization, these traits are more essential than ever.

A new curriculum that prioritizes character education alongside knowledge acquisition recognizes that students are not simply vessels to be filled with information, but complex individuals with unique strengths, weaknesses, and aspirations. It seeks to nurture their intellectual curiosity, creativity, and critical thinking skills while also fostering their emotional intelligence, social awareness, and ethical compass.

This approach involves a fundamental rethinking of what we teach and how we teach it. Instead of focusing solely on academic subjects, the new curriculum incorporates character education into every aspect of the learning experience. Teachers become facilitators of learning, guiding students to explore their values, beliefs, and identities. They encourage students to ask questions, challenge assumptions, and engage in meaningful dialogue with their peers.

The new curriculum also emphasizes experiential learning, providing students with opportunities to apply their knowledge and skills in real-world contexts. Through service learning projects, internships, and community engagement initiatives, students develop a sense of social responsibility and a deeper understanding of the world around them. They learn to collaborate with others, solve problems creatively, and make ethical decisions that impact their communities and the environment.

In this new curriculum, assessment goes beyond standardized tests and grades. It focuses on measuring students' growth in character traits, such as empathy, resilience, and leadership. Teachers use a variety of assessment tools, including self-reflection journals, peer feedback, and portfolios, to gain a holistic understanding of each student's development. This approach not only provides a more accurate picture of student learning but also encourages students to take ownership of their own growth and development.

The benefits of teaching character alongside knowledge are numerous. Students who have been exposed to character education are more likely to exhibit prosocial behavior, engage in civic activities, and make ethical choices in their personal and professional lives. They are better equipped to navigate complex moral dilemmas, resolve conflicts peacefully, and contribute to a more just and equitable society. Moreover, character education can have a positive impact on students' mental and emotional well-being. By cultivating self-awareness, empathy, and a sense of purpose, it can reduce stress, anxiety, and depression, fostering resilience and overall life satisfaction.

The implementation of a new curriculum that teaches character alongside knowledge is not without its challenges. It requires a fundamental shift in mindset among educators, parents, and policymakers. It also necessitates a commitment to professional development and ongoing support for teachers. However, the potential rewards are significant. By investing in the character development of our students, we are investing in the future of our society.

This new curriculum represents a bold vision for education, one that recognizes the interconnectedness of knowledge and character. It is a call to action for educators, policymakers, and communities to work together to create learning environments that nurture the whole child, preparing them not only for academic success but also for a life of purpose, meaning, and ethical decision-making. In a world that is becoming increasingly complex and interconnected, the ability to think critically, act compassionately, and make ethical choices is more important than ever. By teaching character alongside knowledge, we are empowering the next generation to build a better future for themselves and for the world.

ᐅᐅᐅ

The pursuit of academic excellence is admirable, but it is incomplete without the cultivation of ethical values. Let us strive to create schools where students learn not only to succeed but also to serve. Remember, true success is not measured by grades alone, but by the positive impact we have on the world.

FOUR

FROM COMPETITION TO COLLABORATION: RETHINKING SCHOOL CULTURE

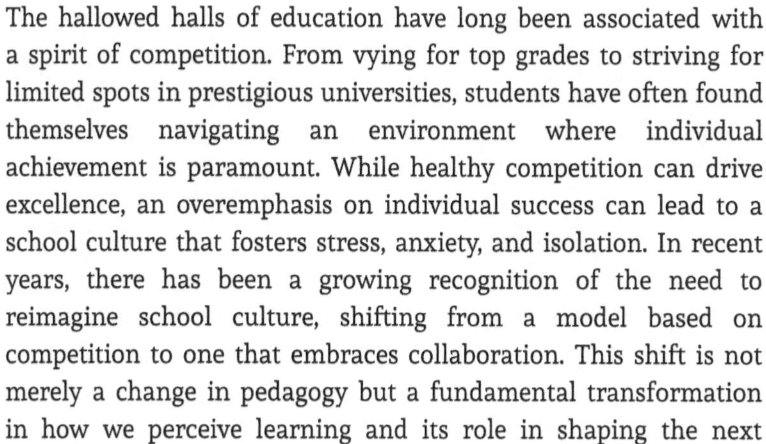

The hallowed halls of education have long been associated with a spirit of competition. From vying for top grades to striving for limited spots in prestigious universities, students have often found themselves navigating an environment where individual achievement is paramount. While healthy competition can drive excellence, an overemphasis on individual success can lead to a school culture that fosters stress, anxiety, and isolation. In recent years, there has been a growing recognition of the need to reimagine school culture, shifting from a model based on competition to one that embraces collaboration. This shift is not merely a change in pedagogy but a fundamental transformation in how we perceive learning and its role in shaping the next generation.

The traditional model of education, often referred to as the "factory model," views students as passive recipients of knowledge, whose success is measured by their ability to outperform their peers. This model has been criticized for its emphasis on standardized testing, its disregard for individual learning styles, and its tendency to stifle creativity and critical thinking. In such an environment, students are often pitted against each other, competing for grades, recognition, and limited resources. This can lead to a sense of isolation, anxiety, and even animosity among students.

In contrast, a collaborative school culture emphasizes the importance of teamwork, cooperation, and mutual support. It recognizes that learning is a social process, where students learn not only from their teachers but also from each other. In a collaborative environment, students are encouraged to share ideas, work together on projects, and support each other in their learning journeys. This not only fosters a sense of community and belonging but also prepares students for the collaborative nature of the modern workplace.

The benefits of a collaborative school culture are numerous. Studies have shown that students who learn in collaborative environments tend to have higher levels of academic achievement, greater self-esteem, and stronger social skills. They are also more likely to be engaged in their learning, to persist in the face of challenges, and to develop a lifelong love of learning. Moreover, a collaborative culture can foster a more positive and inclusive school climate, where all students feel valued and supported.

The shift from competition to collaboration requires a fundamental rethinking of the role of the teacher. In a collaborative classroom, the teacher acts as a facilitator, guiding students in their learning but also encouraging them to take ownership of their education. Teachers create opportunities for students to work together on projects, to share their ideas, and to learn from each other's strengths. They also provide feedback that is constructive and supportive, helping students to identify their areas for growth and to develop strategies for improvement.

Creating a collaborative school culture also involves rethinking the physical space of the school. Traditional classrooms, with their rows of desks facing the front of the room, are designed for lecture-based instruction and individual work. In contrast, collaborative classrooms are flexible and adaptable, with furniture that can be easily rearranged to facilitate group work and discussion. Technology can also play a role in fostering collaboration, with tools such as online forums and shared documents enabling students to collaborate on projects from anywhere in the world.

The shift from competition to collaboration is not without its challenges. It requires a change in mindset among educators, students, and parents. Some teachers may be resistant to relinquishing control and adopting a more facilitative role. Some students may be accustomed to competing with their peers and may find it difficult to adjust to a collaborative environment. Parents may also need to be educated about the benefits of collaboration and how it can support their child's learning.

Despite these challenges, the potential rewards of a collaborative school culture are significant. By fostering a sense of community, belonging, and mutual support, schools can create an environment where all students can thrive. They can prepare students for the collaborative nature of the modern workplace and for the challenges of a rapidly changing world. Moreover, they can instill in students the values of cooperation, empathy, and social responsibility, values that are essential for building a more just and equitable society. The transition from competition to collaboration is not merely a pedagogical shift; it is a profound transformation in how we perceive learning and its role in shaping the next generation.

In conclusion, rethinking school culture from a model based on competition to one that embraces collaboration represents a paradigm shift in education. By fostering a sense of community, encouraging teamwork, and valuing diverse perspectives, schools can create an environment where all students can thrive. This shift requires a change in mindset among educators, students, and parents, as well as a rethinking of the physical space of the school and the use of technology. However, the potential benefits are significant, not only for individual students but also for society as a whole. By embracing collaboration, we can prepare the next generation to be not only successful but also compassionate, engaged, and responsible citizens of the world.

ppp

In an interconnected world, global citizenship is no longer a luxury, but a necessity. By fostering cross-cultural understanding and promoting ethical decision-making, we can empower students to address global challenges and build a more just and sustainable world. Let us remember that we are all connected, and our actions have ripple effects that extend far beyond our borders.

FIVE

Moral Dilemmas: Preparing Students for Real-World Challenges

Life is a series of choices, and many of those choices involve navigating complex moral dilemmas. From personal relationships to professional decisions, individuals constantly face situations where values clash, and there are no easy answers. Preparing students to confront these real-world challenges is a crucial aspect of education that extends beyond the confines of textbooks and standardized tests. By equipping students with the tools to analyze moral dilemmas, make informed decisions, and justify their choices, we empower them to become responsible, ethical, and engaged citizens.

Moral dilemmas are situations where individuals must choose between two or more conflicting moral principles. These dilemmas often involve competing values, such as honesty versus loyalty, individual rights versus the greater good, or justice versus mercy. There are no easy answers to moral dilemmas, as each choice may have both positive and negative consequences. The ability to grapple with these complexities and make thoughtful decisions is essential for navigating the challenges of the real world.

Traditional education often focuses on imparting knowledge and skills, but it may neglect the development of moral reasoning. Students may learn about historical events, scientific principles, and mathematical formulas, but they may not be equipped to apply these concepts to real-world ethical dilemmas. To address this gap, educators are increasingly incorporating moral dilemma discussions and activities into the curriculum.

One approach to teaching moral dilemmas is to present students with hypothetical scenarios that require them to weigh competing values and make difficult choices. For example, students may be asked to consider whether it is ethical to lie to protect a friend, to break a rule for a good cause, or to prioritize their own needs over those of others. These scenarios can spark lively discussions and debates, encouraging students to think critically about their own values and beliefs.

Another approach is to use real-world examples of moral dilemmas. This could involve discussing current events, historical events, or even personal experiences. By analyzing these examples, students can gain a deeper understanding of the complexities of moral decision-making and the potential consequences of their choices.

The goal of teaching moral dilemmas is not to provide students with a set of predetermined answers but to equip them with the skills and knowledge to make informed and ethical decisions. This involves developing their critical thinking skills, their ability to analyze different perspectives, and their capacity for empathy and compassion. It also involves teaching them about different ethical frameworks, such as deontology, consequentialism, and virtue ethics, which can provide them with different lenses through which to view moral dilemmas.

One of the key benefits of teaching moral dilemmas is that it encourages students to think for themselves and to take ownership of their own values. By engaging in discussions and debates, students are exposed to a variety of perspectives and challenged to articulate their own beliefs. This can help them to develop a stronger sense of self-awareness and a deeper understanding of their own moral compass.

Another benefit is that it prepares students for the real-world challenges they will face. Moral dilemmas are not confined to the classroom; they are an integral part of life. By learning to navigate these dilemmas in a safe and supportive environment, students are better equipped to make ethical decisions in their personal and professional lives.

In addition to classroom discussions and activities, there are other ways to incorporate moral dilemma education into the curriculum. For example, schools can invite guest speakers to share their experiences with ethical dilemmas. They can also organize field trips to organizations that deal with ethical issues, such as hospitals, law firms, or non-profit organizations.

The integration of moral dilemma education into the curriculum is not without its challenges. Some educators may be hesitant to tackle controversial topics or to allow students to express dissenting opinions. Others may lack the training or resources to effectively facilitate discussions on ethical issues. However, the potential benefits of this approach are too significant to ignore.

In conclusion, preparing students for real-world challenges involves more than just imparting knowledge and skills. It requires equipping them with the tools to navigate complex moral dilemmas and make informed, ethical decisions. By incorporating moral dilemma education into the curriculum, educators can empower students to become critical thinkers, compassionate individuals, and responsible citizens who are committed to making a positive difference in the world.

ϼϼϼ

Technology has the power to transform our world, but it also raises ethical dilemmas that we must confront. Let us teach our students to navigate the digital age with wisdom and responsibility, using technology to create positive change and to foster greater understanding. Remember, technology is a tool, and its impact depends on how we use it.

SIX

THE ROLE OF TEACHERS: GUIDING ETHICAL DEVELOPMENT

The role of teachers extends far beyond imparting academic knowledge. They are the architects of young minds, the cultivators of character, and the guides who illuminate the path of ethical development. In a world that is constantly evolving and presenting new challenges, the role of teachers in nurturing ethical values and principles in students is more crucial than ever.

Teachers are not merely instructors but also role models. Their actions, words, and attitudes have a profound impact on the ethical development of their students. When teachers demonstrate integrity, respect, and compassion, they create a classroom environment where these values are valued and practiced.

Students learn by observing and emulating the behavior of their teachers, and the ethical principles they witness in the classroom can shape their own moral compasses for years to come.

Guiding ethical development is not a simple task. It requires teachers to possess a deep understanding of ethical theories, principles, and values. They must be able to identify and address ethical dilemmas that arise in the classroom and in the wider world. Teachers also need to be skilled in facilitating discussions and debates on ethical issues, encouraging students to think critically and articulate their own beliefs and values.

One of the key ways in which teachers can guide ethical development is by creating a safe and inclusive learning environment. This means fostering a classroom culture where all students feel valued, respected, and heard. It also means creating opportunities for students to express their opinions, even if those opinions differ from those of their peers or teachers.

When students feel safe to express themselves, they are more likely to engage in meaningful discussions about ethical issues and to develop their own moral reasoning skills.

Another important aspect of guiding ethical development is to provide students with opportunities to practice ethical decision-making. This can be done through role-playing activities, case studies, and simulations. Teachers can also encourage students to participate in service learning projects, where they can apply their knowledge and skills to real-world problems and learn about the ethical implications of their actions.

Teaching ethical decision-making is not about providing students with a set of predetermined answers. Rather, it is about equipping them with the tools to analyze complex ethical dilemmas, weigh competing values, and make informed choices.

This involves teaching them about different ethical frameworks, such as deontology, consequentialism, and virtue ethics, and encouraging them to consider the perspectives of all stakeholders involved.

Teachers can also foster ethical development by integrating ethical considerations into the curriculum. This can be done by discussing the ethical implications of scientific discoveries, historical events, and literary works. For example, a science teacher might discuss the ethical implications of genetic engineering, while a history teacher might explore the ethical dilemmas faced by leaders during times of war.

In addition to their role in the classroom, teachers can also play a vital role in shaping school culture. By promoting a culture of respect, inclusivity, and social responsibility, teachers can create a learning environment that supports ethical development.

This can involve organizing school-wide events that celebrate diversity, encouraging students to participate in community service projects, and creating opportunities for students to share their experiences with ethical dilemmas.

The role of teachers in guiding ethical development is not without its challenges. Teachers may face resistance from students who are uncomfortable discussing controversial topics or who have different values than their own. They may also feel pressure from parents or administrators to avoid controversial issues or to promote a particular set of values.

However, these challenges should not deter teachers from their commitment to fostering ethical development in their students.

By creating a safe and inclusive learning environment, providing opportunities for students to practice ethical decision-making, integrating ethical considerations into the curriculum, and shaping school culture, teachers can empower students to become responsible, ethical, and engaged citizens.

In a world that is increasingly complex and interconnected, the ability to think critically, act compassionately, and make ethical choices is more important than ever. Teachers have a unique opportunity to shape the future by guiding the ethical development of the next generation.

ᐅᐅᐅ

Environmental responsibility is not just about protecting nature; it's about safeguarding our future. Let us educate our students about the interconnectedness of all living things and empower them to become stewards of the planet. Remember, we are not separate from nature; we are a part of it.

SEVEN

PARENTS AS PARTNERS: SUPPORTING VALUES AT HOME AND SCHOOL

The adage "it takes a village to raise a child" holds true in the realm of values education. While schools play a crucial role in instilling ethical principles and moral values in students, the involvement of parents as partners is equally vital. The home environment is where children first learn about right and wrong, where they observe and internalize the values that shape their character.

By working together, parents and schools can create a cohesive and consistent approach to values education, ensuring that children receive a strong foundation in ethics that will guide them throughout their lives.

Parents are the primary role models for their children. The values they exhibit in their daily lives, the way they treat others, and the choices they make all leave a lasting impression on their children. Children learn by observing and imitating their parents, and the values they see modeled at home are often the ones they internalize most deeply. Therefore, parents have a unique opportunity to instill values such as honesty, respect, responsibility, compassion, and fairness in their children from a young age.

Creating a home environment that supports values education involves more than just talking about values. It requires parents to actively model those values in their own behavior. This means being honest and truthful, treating others with respect and kindness, taking responsibility for one's actions, showing compassion for those in need, and being fair and just in one's dealings with others. When children see their parents living by these values, they are more likely to adopt them as their own.

In addition to modeling values, parents can also actively teach their children about ethics and morality. This can be done through conversations, stories, and real-life examples. Parents can discuss ethical dilemmas with their children, encouraging them to think critically about different perspectives and to consider the consequences of their choices.

They can also share stories about historical figures or fictional characters who embody certain values, and they can point out examples of ethical behavior in their own lives or in the lives of others.

Beyond the home environment, parents can also play an active role in supporting values education at school. This can involve volunteering in the classroom, participating in school events, and communicating regularly with teachers. By building strong relationships with teachers, parents can gain a better understanding of the school's values curriculum and how they can reinforce those values at home. They can also provide teachers with insights into their child's unique strengths and challenges, allowing teachers to tailor their approach to meet the individual needs of each student.

Parents can also support values education by creating opportunities for their children to practice ethical decision-making outside of school. This can involve encouraging them to participate in community service projects, volunteer work, or extracurricular activities that promote social responsibility and civic engagement.

These experiences not only allow children to apply their values in real-world contexts but also help them develop a sense of empathy and compassion for others.

Of course, the partnership between parents and schools is not always smooth sailing. There may be times when parents and teachers have different perspectives on values education or disagree on how best to address a particular issue. However, open communication and mutual respect are essential for building a strong partnership that benefits all students.

Parents and teachers should be encouraged to communicate openly with each other, to share their concerns and perspectives, and to work together to find solutions that are in the best interests of the child.

In conclusion, parents play a crucial role in supporting values education, both at home and at school. By modeling values, actively teaching ethics and morality, building strong relationships with teachers, and creating opportunities for their children to practice ethical decision-making, parents can help ensure that their children receive a strong foundation in ethics that will guide them throughout their lives. The partnership between parents and schools is essential for creating a cohesive and consistent approach to values education, one that prepares students to navigate the complexities of the modern world with integrity, compassion, and a strong sense of social responsibility.

ꗞꗞꗞ

Diversity is a gift that enriches our lives and our communities. Let us celebrate our differences and create inclusive learning environments where all voices are valued. Remember, our strength lies in our diversity, and our unity lies in our shared humanity.

EIGHT

COMMUNITY CONNECTIONS: LEARNING BEYOND THE CLASSROOM WALLS

Education, in its truest form, is not confined to the four walls of a classroom. It is a lifelong journey that extends into the community, where real-world experiences shape values, perspectives, and a deeper understanding of the world. Community connections are an integral part of this journey, enriching the educational experience and fostering a sense of social responsibility in students. By venturing beyond the classroom walls, students are exposed to diverse perspectives, gain practical skills, and develop a deeper understanding of their role in society.

The traditional model of education, with its emphasis on standardized testing and academic achievement, often overlooks the importance of community engagement. However, a growing body of research suggests that students who are actively involved in their communities tend to have higher academic achievement, stronger social skills, and a greater sense of civic responsibility.

They are also more likely to be engaged in their learning, to persist in the face of challenges, and to pursue higher education.

Community connections can take many forms. They can involve volunteering at local organizations, participating in community events, or simply interacting with people from different backgrounds. These experiences expose students to diverse perspectives, challenge their assumptions, and broaden their understanding of the world.

They also provide opportunities for students to apply their knowledge and skills in real-world contexts, gaining valuable experience and building confidence in their abilities.

One of the key benefits of community connections is that they foster a sense of social responsibility in students. By working with others to address community needs, students learn the importance of collaboration, empathy, and civic engagement. They also develop a deeper understanding of the challenges facing their communities and the role they can play in creating positive change.

Community connections can also have a significant impact on students' academic achievement. By applying their knowledge and skills in real-world contexts, students gain a deeper understanding of academic concepts and their relevance to their lives. They also develop critical thinking skills, problem-solving abilities, and the ability to communicate effectively with diverse audiences.

Moreover, community connections can provide students with access to resources and opportunities that may not be available in the classroom. For example, students who volunteer at local organizations may have the chance to learn from experts in their fields, to network with professionals, and to gain exposure to different career paths.

These experiences can help students make informed decisions about their future and prepare them for success in the workforce.

The benefits of community connections are not limited to students. Communities also benefit from the energy, enthusiasm, and fresh perspectives that students bring. By engaging with students, community organizations can tap into a valuable source of talent and ideas. They can also build stronger relationships with schools and families, creating a more supportive and collaborative environment for all.

Creating meaningful community connections requires a concerted effort on the part of schools, families, and community organizations. Schools can play a leading role by incorporating community engagement into the curriculum, providing opportunities for students to volunteer, and partnering with local organizations. Families can support their children's community involvement by encouraging them to participate in volunteer activities, attending community events together, and discussing the importance of social responsibility.

Community organizations can also play a role by welcoming student volunteers, providing mentorship opportunities, and working with schools to develop mutually beneficial partnerships.

In conclusion, learning beyond the classroom walls is essential for the holistic development of students. By forging strong community connections, students gain valuable experiences, develop essential skills, and cultivate a sense of social responsibility. These connections enrich the educational experience, prepare students for success in the workforce, and contribute to the well-being of the community.

By working together, schools, families, and community organizations can create a vibrant ecosystem of learning that extends beyond the classroom walls and prepares students for a life of purpose, meaning, and impact.

❦❦❦

Social justice is not just an ideal; it's a call to action. Let us empower students to challenge injustice, advocate for marginalized groups, and create a more equitable world. Remember, our silence is complicity, and our actions can make a difference.

NINE

GLOBAL CITIZENSHIP: ETHICS IN AN INTERCONNECTED WORLD

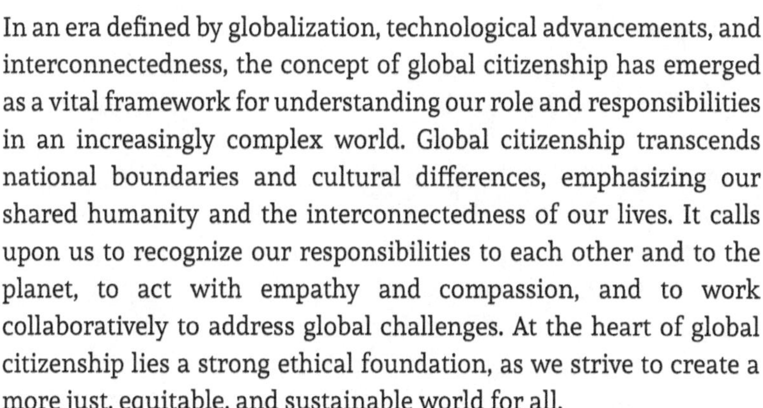

In an era defined by globalization, technological advancements, and interconnectedness, the concept of global citizenship has emerged as a vital framework for understanding our role and responsibilities in an increasingly complex world. Global citizenship transcends national boundaries and cultural differences, emphasizing our shared humanity and the interconnectedness of our lives. It calls upon us to recognize our responsibilities to each other and to the planet, to act with empathy and compassion, and to work collaboratively to address global challenges. At the heart of global citizenship lies a strong ethical foundation, as we strive to create a more just, equitable, and sustainable world for all.

The concept of global citizenship is not new. Throughout history, philosophers, religious leaders, and social activists have advocated for a broader sense of community and responsibility that extends beyond one's own tribe, nation, or culture. However, the advent of globalization, with its rapid flow of information, goods, and people across borders, has intensified the need for a global perspective. We are now more interconnected than ever before, with our actions having ripple effects that can be felt across the globe.

Global citizenship is not about denying one's own cultural identity or national allegiance. Rather, it is about recognizing that we are all part of a larger human family, with shared values and aspirations. It is about understanding that our well-being is inextricably linked to the well-being of others, regardless of where they live or what their background may be.

Ethics plays a central role in global citizenship. Ethical principles, such as respect for human dignity, justice, fairness, and compassion, provide a moral compass that guides our actions and decisions in an interconnected world. As global citizens, we are called upon to act ethically not only towards our fellow citizens but also towards people from other cultures and nations. This means respecting their rights, valuing their perspectives, and working collaboratively to address shared challenges.

In an interconnected world, ethical considerations are paramount. Issues such as climate change, poverty, inequality, conflict, and human rights violations transcend national boundaries and require global solutions. As global citizens, we have a responsibility to educate ourselves about these issues, to engage in dialogue with people from different backgrounds, and to advocate for policies and practices that promote justice, equity, and sustainability.

Education plays a crucial role in fostering global citizenship. By teaching students about different cultures, perspectives, and global issues, we can help them develop a broader understanding of the world and their place in it. We can also encourage them to think critically about global challenges, to explore different solutions, and to take action to make a positive difference in the world.

Global citizenship education should not be limited to the classroom. It should permeate all aspects of the educational experience, from extracurricular activities to community engagement initiatives. Schools can partner with international organizations, participate in exchange programs, and leverage technology to connect students with peers from around the world. By fostering cross-cultural understanding and collaboration, we can prepare students to become responsible global citizens who are equipped to address the challenges of the 21st century.

The benefits of global citizenship are numerous. Individuals who embrace a global perspective are more likely to be open-minded, tolerant, and empathetic. They are better equipped to navigate a diverse and interconnected world, to build bridges across cultures, and to work collaboratively to solve global problems. Moreover, global citizenship can contribute to personal growth and well-being, as individuals gain a deeper understanding of themselves and their place in the world.

In conclusion, global citizenship is an essential framework for understanding our role and responsibilities in an interconnected world. It calls upon us to act with empathy, compassion, and a sense of shared responsibility towards each other and the planet. Ethics is at the heart of global citizenship, providing a moral compass that guides our actions and decisions. Education plays a crucial role in fostering global citizenship, equipping students with the knowledge, skills, and values needed to navigate a complex and interconnected world. By embracing global citizenship, we can create a more just, equitable, and sustainable future for all.

ppp

Mindfulness and well-being are essential for navigating the complexities of modern life. Let us teach our students to cultivate inner peace, emotional resilience, and compassion for themselves and others. Remember, true happiness comes not from external achievements but from inner peace.

TEN

TECHNOLOGY AND ETHICS: NAVIGATING THE DIGITAL AGE

The digital age, an era characterized by the rapid advancement of technology, has brought about unprecedented changes in how we live, work, and interact with one another. While these advancements have undoubtedly improved our lives in many ways, they have also raised a plethora of ethical questions and challenges. Navigating the ethical implications of technology is essential to ensure that technological progress aligns with human values and serves the greater good.

The digital age has brought about a paradigm shift in how we access and share information. The internet has become a vast repository of knowledge, accessible to anyone with a connection. However, the democratization of information has also led to the spread of misinformation, hate speech, and online harassment. As digital citizens, we have an ethical responsibility to be discerning consumers of information, to critically evaluate sources, and to avoid contributing to the spread of harmful content.

Social media platforms have revolutionized communication, connecting people from all corners of the globe. However, these platforms have also been used to manipulate public opinion, spread propaganda, and incite violence. The algorithms that power social media can create filter bubbles, where individuals are only exposed to information that confirms their existing biases. This can lead to polarization and a breakdown of civil discourse. As users of social media, we have an ethical responsibility to be mindful of the impact of our words and actions, to seek out diverse perspectives, and to engage in respectful dialogue.

Artificial intelligence (AI) is poised to transform many aspects of our lives, from healthcare to transportation to education. However, the development and deployment of AI raise ethical concerns about bias, discrimination, and job displacement. AI algorithms are often trained on biased data, which can lead to discriminatory outcomes. For example, facial recognition technology has been shown to be less accurate for people with darker skin tones. As developers and users of AI, we have an ethical responsibility to ensure that AI systems are fair, transparent, and accountable.

The rise of the gig economy, fueled by digital platforms, has provided new opportunities for flexible work. However, it has also raised concerns about worker rights, job security, and fair compensation. Gig workers often lack access to benefits such as health insurance and paid time off, and they may be vulnerable to exploitation by platform companies. As consumers of gig economy services, we have an ethical responsibility to support fair labor practices and to advocate for the rights of gig workers.

Privacy is another major ethical concern in the digital age. The vast amounts of data collected by companies and governments can be used to track our movements, monitor our behavior, and even predict our preferences. This data can be used for benign purposes, such as targeted advertising, but it can also be used for nefarious purposes, such as discrimination or surveillance. As digital citizens, we have an ethical responsibility to protect our privacy, to be mindful of the data we share, and to advocate for stronger privacy protections.

The digital age also presents challenges to traditional notions of intellectual property. The ease with which digital content can be copied and shared has led to widespread copyright infringement. At the same time, the open-source movement has demonstrated the power of collaboration and the potential for innovation when knowledge is freely shared. As creators and consumers of digital content, we have an ethical responsibility to respect intellectual property rights while also supporting open access to knowledge.

Navigating the ethical implications of technology requires a multi-faceted approach. Education plays a crucial role in raising awareness of ethical issues and empowering individuals to make informed decisions. Schools, universities, and community organizations should offer courses and workshops on digital ethics, teaching students about the potential risks and benefits of technology and how to use it responsibly.

Policymakers also have a crucial role to play. They need to develop regulations that protect privacy, ensure fairness, and promote accountability in the development and deployment of technology. They also need to invest in research and development to address the ethical challenges of emerging technologies such as AI and biotechnology.

Ultimately, the responsibility for navigating the ethical implications of technology rests with each of us. As digital citizens, we have a duty to use technology responsibly, to be mindful of its impact on ourselves and others, and to advocate for a digital future that aligns with our values and aspirations. By working together, we can ensure that technological progress serves the greater good and contributes to a more just, equitable, and sustainable world.

ᐅᐅᐅ

Creativity and imagination are powerful forces that can shape the world. Let us encourage our students to explore their creativity and to use their imagination to envision a better future. Remember, the most innovative solutions often come from the most unexpected places.

ELEVEN

Environmental Responsibility: Educating for a Sustainable Future

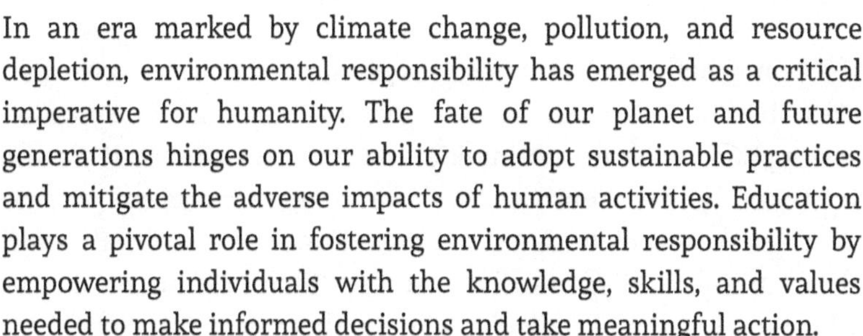

In an era marked by climate change, pollution, and resource depletion, environmental responsibility has emerged as a critical imperative for humanity. The fate of our planet and future generations hinges on our ability to adopt sustainable practices and mitigate the adverse impacts of human activities. Education plays a pivotal role in fostering environmental responsibility by empowering individuals with the knowledge, skills, and values needed to make informed decisions and take meaningful action.

Environmental education goes beyond imparting knowledge about ecological systems and environmental issues. It is about cultivating a deep understanding of our interconnectedness with the natural world and fostering a sense of stewardship for the planet. It is about empowering individuals to become agents of change, capable of making informed decisions that prioritize sustainability and environmental well-being.

At its core, environmental education is about raising awareness. It involves informing individuals about the complex environmental challenges we face, such as climate change, pollution, deforestation, and loss of biodiversity. It also involves educating individuals about the root causes of these problems, such as unsustainable consumption patterns, overpopulation, and inequitable distribution of resources. By raising awareness, environmental education can spark a sense of urgency and inspire individuals to take action.

Beyond awareness, environmental education focuses on building knowledge and understanding. It delves into the science behind environmental issues, exploring the complex interactions between human activities and the natural world. It teaches students about ecological principles, biodiversity, climate change, and sustainable resource management. By equipping individuals with a solid foundation in environmental science, education can empower them to make informed decisions and advocate for sustainable solutions.

Environmental education also emphasizes the development of critical thinking skills. It encourages students to question assumptions, analyze information, and evaluate evidence. It teaches them to think systematically about complex problems and to consider the social, economic, and environmental implications of their decisions. By fostering critical thinking, environmental education empowers individuals to become discerning consumers of information and to make informed choices that prioritize sustainability.

Values play a central role in environmental education. It instills a sense of respect for the natural world, a recognition of our interdependence with other species, and a commitment to protecting the planet for future generations. It teaches students about the ethical dimensions of environmental issues, such as the rights of future generations, the intrinsic value of nature, and the responsibility of developed nations to assist developing nations in achieving sustainable development.

Environmental education is not confined to the classroom. It extends into the community, where students can engage in hands-on activities, such as tree planting, community gardening, and waste reduction initiatives. These experiences not only deepen their understanding of environmental issues but also foster a sense of ownership and empowerment. By taking action in their own communities, students can see the tangible impact of their efforts and feel a sense of pride in contributing to a sustainable future.

The integration of environmental education into the curriculum is essential for preparing students for the challenges of the 21st century. By equipping them with knowledge, skills, and values, we can empower them to become responsible environmental stewards. Environmental education should be a lifelong endeavor, starting in early childhood and continuing throughout adulthood. By investing in environmental education, we are investing in the future of our planet and ensuring a sustainable future for generations to come.

The importance of environmental responsibility and education for a sustainable future cannot be overstated. The challenges we face are complex and multifaceted, requiring collective action and a fundamental shift in our relationship with the natural world. By empowering individuals with the knowledge, skills, and values needed to make informed decisions and take meaningful action, environmental education can play a pivotal role in shaping a more sustainable and equitable future for all.

❧❧❧

Leadership is not about power and control; it's about service and empowerment. Let us inspire our students to become leaders who serve others and who work towards the betterment of society. Remember, true leaders are those who inspire others to be their best selves.

TWELVE

DIVERSITY AND INCLUSION: VALUING ALL VOICES

In a world that is becoming increasingly interconnected and diverse, the concepts of diversity and inclusion have taken center stage. These concepts go beyond mere tolerance of differences; they embrace and celebrate the richness that diversity brings to our lives. Valuing all voices means recognizing that every individual, regardless of their background, has something unique and valuable to contribute. It means creating a space where everyone feels seen, heard, and valued for who they are.

Diversity encompasses a wide range of human experiences, including race, ethnicity, gender, sexual orientation, age, religion, socioeconomic status, and ability. It is the mosaic of human differences that enriches our communities, workplaces, and institutions. When we value diversity, we acknowledge that these differences are not obstacles to overcome, but rather strengths to be leveraged.

Inclusion, on the other hand, refers to the active creation of an environment where everyone feels welcome and included. It is about ensuring that everyone has equal opportunities to participate, contribute, and succeed. Inclusion is not simply about inviting diverse individuals to the table; it is about creating a space where everyone feels comfortable sharing their perspectives and where their voices are heard and valued.

Valuing all voices is not just a moral imperative; it is also a practical necessity. When we exclude certain voices from the conversation, we miss out on valuable insights and perspectives. We risk making decisions that are based on incomplete or biased information. By valuing all voices, we can tap into the collective wisdom of our communities and make better decisions that benefit everyone.

In the context of education, valuing all voices means creating a learning environment where every student feels seen, heard, and valued. It means recognizing that students come from diverse backgrounds and have different learning styles, interests, and needs. It means providing all students with equitable access to resources and opportunities, regardless of their background or circumstances.

Teachers play a crucial role in valuing all voices in the classroom. They can create a safe and inclusive space by setting clear expectations for respectful behavior, modeling inclusive language, and celebrating diversity in their curriculum and teaching practices. They can also create opportunities for students to share their perspectives through discussions, group work, and presentations.

Beyond the classroom, schools can foster a culture of diversity and inclusion by offering diverse extracurricular activities, celebrating cultural events, and providing resources for students from underrepresented groups. They can also work to eliminate bias and discrimination in their policies and practices.

Valuing all voices is not only important for individual students; it is also essential for the health of our communities and society as a whole. When we create inclusive communities where everyone feels valued, we foster a sense of belonging and connection. We build stronger social bonds and reduce conflict. We also create a more vibrant and dynamic society, where innovation and creativity flourish.

In the workplace, valuing all voices is essential for creating a productive and engaging work environment. When employees feel valued and included, they are more likely to be motivated, engaged, and committed to their work. They are also more likely to share their ideas and perspectives, which can lead to better decision-making and innovation.

To create a more inclusive workplace, organizations can implement diversity and inclusion training programs, create employee resource groups, and establish mentorship programs. They can also review their hiring and promotion practices to ensure that they are fair and equitable.

Valuing all voices is an ongoing process that requires continuous effort and commitment. It is about challenging our own biases and assumptions, listening to others with empathy and respect, and creating spaces where everyone feels safe to share their experiences and perspectives. When we value all voices, we create a more just, equitable, and inclusive world for everyone.

In conclusion, diversity and inclusion are not just buzzwords; they are fundamental principles that should guide our interactions with one another. Valuing all voices means recognizing the unique contributions that each individual brings to the table. It means creating a space where everyone feels seen, heard, and valued for who they are. By valuing all voices, we can build stronger communities, create more innovative workplaces, and foster a more just and equitable society.

ᐁᐁᐁ

The arts and culture are not just forms of entertainment; they are powerful tools for ethical expression and social commentary. Let us encourage our students to engage with the arts and culture and to use their creative voices to challenge injustice and inspire change. Remember, art has the power to move hearts and minds in ways that words alone cannot.

THIRTEEN

Social Justice: Empowering Students to Make a Difference

The concept of social justice has long been a driving force for positive change in societies around the world. It is the pursuit of fairness, equity, and equality for all members of a community, regardless of their background, identity, or circumstances. In the context of education, social justice goes beyond simply teaching students about the ideals of fairness and equality; it involves empowering them to actively challenge injustice, advocate for marginalized groups, and create a more equitable world.

Education plays a pivotal role in shaping the values and beliefs of future generations. By introducing students to the concepts of social justice, educators can ignite a passion for social change and equip them with the tools to make a difference.

It is through education that young people learn about the systemic inequalities that persist in society, the historical struggles for justice, and the ongoing efforts to create a more inclusive world.

Empowering students to make a difference begins with critical consciousness-raising. This involves helping students to understand the root causes of social injustice, such as racism, sexism, poverty, and discrimination. It also involves encouraging them to question societal norms and power structures that perpetuate inequality.

By developing critical consciousness, students become aware of their own social location and the privileges or disadvantages they may experience based on their identity.

Once students have developed a critical awareness of social injustice, they can be empowered to take action. This can involve participating in advocacy campaigns, volunteering for community organizations, or organizing protests and demonstrations. Students can also use their voices to speak out against injustice, whether through writing letters to elected officials, creating social media campaigns, or simply engaging in conversations with friends and family.

Empowering students to make a difference also involves teaching them the skills they need to be effective advocates for change. This includes critical thinking skills, communication skills, and problem-solving skills. Students need to be able to research and analyze complex social issues, communicate their ideas clearly and persuasively, and work collaboratively with others to develop and implement solutions.

Schools can play a crucial role in empowering students to make a difference by creating a supportive and inclusive learning environment. This involves fostering a culture of respect for diversity, encouraging open dialogue and debate, and providing opportunities for students to explore social justice issues in a safe and supportive setting.

Schools can also offer extracurricular activities, such as social justice clubs or volunteer programs, that provide students with opportunities to put their values into action.

Teachers are also essential to empowering students for social change. They can serve as role models by demonstrating a commitment to social justice in their own lives and by creating a classroom environment that values diversity and encourages critical thinking.

Teachers can also incorporate social justice themes into their curriculum, using real-world examples to illustrate the impact of inequality and the importance of social action.

The benefits of empowering students to make a difference are far-reaching. Students who are engaged in social justice issues are more likely to be active and informed citizens, to participate in civic life, and to make a positive contribution to their communities.

They are also more likely to be empathetic, compassionate, and understanding of others, regardless of their background or circumstances.

Empowering students to make a difference is not only beneficial for individuals and communities; it is also essential for the future of our planet. The challenges we face, such as climate change, poverty, and inequality, require collective action and a commitment to social justice. By empowering young people to become agents of change, we are investing in a more just, equitable, and sustainable future for all.

In conclusion, empowering students to make a difference is a critical aspect of education in the 21st century. By fostering critical consciousness, teaching advocacy skills, and creating a supportive learning environment, educators can ignite a passion for social justice in young people and equip them to create a more equitable and inclusive world.

The challenges we face are complex and multifaceted, but by empowering the next generation to take action, we can build a brighter future for all.

ᐅᐅᐅ

Assessment and evaluation should not just measure academic achievement; they should also gauge ethical growth and character development. Let us develop holistic assessment methods that capture the full range of human potential. Remember, education is not just about preparing students for tests; it's about preparing them for life.

FOURTEEN

MINDFULNESS AND WELL-BEING: CULTIVATING INNER PEACE

In a world characterized by constant stimuli, relentless demands, and an ever-accelerating pace of life, finding inner peace has become an elusive yet essential pursuit. The relentless pursuit of external achievements and material possessions often leaves individuals feeling empty and unfulfilled. It is in this context that mindfulness and well-being have emerged as powerful tools for cultivating inner peace, fostering emotional resilience, and promoting overall well-being.

Mindfulness, at its core, is the practice of paying non-judgmental attention to the present moment. It involves cultivating awareness of our thoughts, emotions, bodily sensations, and the external environment without getting caught up in them.

By anchoring ourselves in the present moment, we can break free from the cycle of rumination about the past and worry about the future, which often fuels stress and anxiety.

The practice of mindfulness has deep roots in ancient contemplative traditions, such as Buddhism and yoga. However, in recent decades, mindfulness has gained widespread recognition and acceptance in secular contexts, such as healthcare, education, and the workplace.

Numerous studies have demonstrated the positive effects of mindfulness on mental and physical health, including reducing stress, anxiety, and depression, improving sleep, and boosting immune function.

Well-being, on the other hand, is a multi-dimensional concept that encompasses physical, mental, emotional, social, and spiritual aspects of life. It is not simply the absence of illness or distress but a state of flourishing, where individuals feel a sense of purpose, meaning, and connection to themselves and others. While external factors such as wealth, status, and relationships can contribute to well-being, true well-being arises from within, from a deep sense of inner peace and contentment.

Cultivating inner peace through mindfulness and well-being is a journey that requires commitment, patience, and self-compassion. It involves developing a regular mindfulness practice, such as meditation, yoga, or mindful movement. These practices help to quiet the mind, cultivate awareness of the present moment, and develop a non-reactive stance towards thoughts and emotions.

In addition to formal mindfulness practices, cultivating inner peace also involves integrating mindfulness into our daily lives. This can be done by paying attention to our everyday activities, such as eating, walking, or washing dishes, with full awareness.

It can also involve taking breaks throughout the day to simply pause, breathe, and connect with the present moment.

The benefits of cultivating inner peace are profound. Individuals who practice mindfulness and prioritize well-being tend to experience lower levels of stress, anxiety, and depression. They are more resilient in the face of challenges, more compassionate towards themselves and others, and more appreciative of the simple joys of life. They are also more likely to experience positive emotions such as joy, gratitude, and love.

Moreover, cultivating inner peace can have a ripple effect, not only on individuals but also on their relationships and communities. When individuals are at peace with themselves, they are more likely to be patient, understanding, and supportive of others. They are also more likely to engage in prosocial behavior and to contribute to the well-being of their communities.

In the context of education, cultivating inner peace through mindfulness and well-being can have a transformative impact on students. By teaching mindfulness practices in schools, educators can help students develop self-awareness, emotional regulation skills, and resilience. This can improve their academic performance, reduce stress and anxiety, and promote overall well-being.

Cultivating inner peace is not a quick fix or a magic bullet. It is an ongoing process that requires dedication and self-compassion. However, the rewards are immeasurable. By embracing mindfulness and prioritizing well-being, we can create a life that is more fulfilling, meaningful, and joyful.

We can find inner peace amidst the chaos of the modern world and live a life that is aligned with our deepest values and aspirations.

In conclusion, the cultivation of inner peace through mindfulness and well-being is essential for navigating the challenges of the modern world and creating a life that is truly fulfilling.

By anchoring ourselves in the present moment, cultivating awareness of our thoughts and emotions, and prioritizing well-being, we can find inner peace amidst the chaos and live a life that is aligned with our deepest values and aspirations.

ƿƿƿ

Reforming Japan's education system is not just about changing policies and practices; it's about transforming our mindset and our culture. Let us embrace innovation, collaboration, and a student-centered approach to learning that prioritizes holistic development. Remember, education is not just about the past or the present; it's about shaping the future.

FIFTEEN

Creativity and Ethics: Exploring the Power of Imagination

Creativity, the wellspring of innovation and artistic expression, is a force that propels humanity forward. It is the ability to generate novel ideas, to forge connections between seemingly disparate concepts, and to envision new possibilities. Imagination, the faculty that allows us to transcend the boundaries of the tangible world, is the driving force behind creativity.

However, as we explore the power of imagination, we must also grapple with the ethical implications that arise when creativity is unleashed. The interplay between creativity and ethics is a complex and nuanced one, with the potential for both great good and great harm.

Creativity, in its purest form, is a celebration of human ingenuity and the boundless potential of the human mind. It is the spark that ignites progress, drives innovation, and enriches our cultural landscape. From the invention of the wheel to the creation of the internet, creativity has been the engine of human advancement.

It is through creative expression that we explore our deepest emotions, challenge societal norms, and envision new possibilities for the future.

Imagination, the cornerstone of creativity, is a faculty that allows us to transcend the limitations of the physical world and to envision what could be. It is the playground of the mind, where ideas are born, nurtured, and transformed into reality. Imagination allows us to empathize with others, to understand different perspectives, and to create worlds that exist only in our minds. It is the source of our dreams, our aspirations, and our hopes for the future.

However, the power of imagination can also be a double-edged sword. While it can be used to create beauty, inspire hope, and promote understanding, it can also be used to manipulate, deceive, and even harm. The ethical implications of creativity are particularly salient in the digital age, where the lines between reality and fiction are increasingly blurred.

The advent of digital technologies has democratized creativity, allowing individuals from all walks of life to express themselves and share their ideas with the world. However, this democratization has also led to the proliferation of misinformation, deepfakes, and other forms of digital manipulation.

The ability to create realistic but false content raises serious ethical concerns about the potential for harm, both to individuals and to society as a whole.

In the realm of art and entertainment, creativity often pushes boundaries and challenges societal norms. While this can be a positive force for social change, it can also lead to controversy and offense. Artists and creators must grapple with the ethical implications of their work, considering the potential impact on their audience and the wider community.

The question of where to draw the line between artistic freedom and social responsibility is a complex one, with no easy answers.

In the business world, creativity is often seen as a key driver of innovation and competitive advantage. However, the pursuit of profit can sometimes lead to unethical practices, such as planned obsolescence, misleading advertising, and exploitation of workers. As consumers, we have an ethical responsibility to support companies that prioritize ethical practices and to hold accountable those that do not.

In the realm of science and technology, creativity is essential for pushing the boundaries of knowledge and developing new solutions to global challenges. However, the potential for misuse of scientific discoveries and technological innovations raises ethical concerns about the impact on human rights, privacy, and the environment. Scientists and engineers must adhere to ethical guidelines and consider the potential consequences of their work.

To navigate the ethical challenges of creativity, we need to develop a framework that balances the freedom of expression with the responsibility to do no harm.

This involves cultivating a critical awareness of the potential impact of our creative endeavors, considering the perspectives of all stakeholders, and adhering to ethical principles such as honesty, fairness, and respect for others.

Education plays a crucial role in fostering ethical creativity. By teaching students about the ethical implications of creativity, encouraging them to think critically about the potential consequences of their actions, and providing them with opportunities to engage in ethical decision-making, we can help them to become responsible and ethical creators.

In conclusion, creativity and ethics are inextricably linked. The power of imagination can be harnessed for both good and ill. By exploring the ethical implications of creativity, we can ensure that our creative endeavors contribute to a more just, equitable, and sustainable world.

❦❦❦

The vision of ethical schools is not a distant dream; it's a tangible goal that we can achieve together. Let us work collaboratively to create schools that nurture values, character, and a sense of social responsibility. Remember, the future of our society depends on the education we provide today.

SIXTEEN

Leadership and Service: Inspiring Future Changemakers

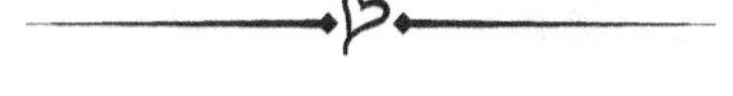

The intertwining concepts of leadership and service hold a unique power to inspire and shape future generations into becoming agents of change. True leadership transcends the mere pursuit of personal gain or power, encompassing a deep-seated commitment to serving others and working towards the betterment of society.

By fostering a culture of leadership and service within educational institutions and communities, we can cultivate a generation of changemakers who are equipped with the skills, values, and passion to address the complex challenges facing our world.

Leadership is often associated with authority and decision-making, but it is fundamentally about inspiring and empowering others to achieve a common goal. A true leader is not simply someone who gives orders, but someone who motivates, guides, and supports others in their pursuit of excellence. In the context of social change, leadership is about envisioning a better future, mobilizing resources and support, and inspiring others to join in the effort to create that future.

Service, on the other hand, is about putting the needs of others before one's own. It is about contributing to the well-being of one's community, country, or the world at large. Service can take many forms, from volunteering at a local soup kitchen to working on a global health initiative.

It is not simply about doing good deeds, but about engaging in meaningful and impactful work that addresses the root causes of social problems.

When leadership and service are combined, they create a powerful force for positive change. Leaders who are committed to service are driven by a deep sense of purpose and a desire to make a difference in the world. They are not afraid to take risks, to challenge the status quo, and to speak out against injustice. They inspire others to join them in their cause, creating a ripple effect that can transform entire communities and even nations.

In the context of education, cultivating leadership and service involves providing students with opportunities to lead and to serve. This can be done through extracurricular activities, such as student government, clubs, and volunteer programs. It can also be done through service learning projects, which integrate academic learning with community service.

By participating in these activities, students develop leadership skills, such as communication, collaboration, and decision-making. They also learn the importance of social responsibility and civic engagement.

Mentorship plays a crucial role in inspiring future changemakers.

Young people need role models who embody the values of leadership and service. Mentors can provide guidance, support, and encouragement to students who are aspiring to make a difference in the world.

They can also share their own experiences and insights, helping students to navigate the challenges and opportunities that lie ahead.

Inspiring future changemakers also involves creating a culture of service within educational institutions and communities. This means valuing and recognizing the contributions of those who serve others. It also means providing resources and support to individuals and organizations that are working to make a positive impact on the world. When young people see that service is valued and supported, they are more likely to embrace it as a way of life.

The benefits of cultivating leadership and service in young people are numerous. Students who are engaged in leadership and service activities are more likely to be successful in school, to graduate from college, and to pursue meaningful careers.

They are also more likely to be active and engaged citizens, to volunteer their time, and to donate to charitable causes.

Moreover, leadership and service can have a profound impact on the personal development of young people. By taking on leadership roles and serving others, students develop self-confidence, empathy, and a sense of purpose.

They also learn the importance of teamwork, collaboration, and social responsibility. These skills and values are essential for success in all aspects of life, from personal relationships to professional careers.

In conclusion, leadership and service are powerful tools for inspiring future changemakers. By fostering a culture of leadership and service within educational institutions and communities, we can empower young people to take on the challenges facing our world and to create a more just, equitable, and sustainable future.

The next generation of leaders will not be defined by their wealth or power, but by their commitment to serving others and making a positive impact on the world. By investing in the leadership and service potential of our young people, we are investing in a brighter future for all.

ᐁᐁᐁ

Education is not a destination; it's a lifelong journey of growth and transformation. Let us instill in our students a love of learning and a commitment to lifelong personal and ethical development. Remember, the most valuable lessons are often learned outside the classroom.

SEVENTEEN

THE ROLE OF ARTS AND CULTURE: NURTURING ETHICAL EXPRESSION

In the tapestry of human experience, arts and culture hold a profound significance, serving as a mirror reflecting society's values, beliefs, and aspirations. They are not merely decorative elements or sources of entertainment; they are powerful tools for nurturing ethical expression, fostering critical thinking, and inspiring empathy and compassion. By recognizing and harnessing the potential of arts and culture, we can create a more ethical and harmonious society.

Arts and culture encompass a wide range of human expressions, including literature, music, visual arts, theater, dance, and film. These creative endeavors offer unique ways of exploring complex themes, challenging social norms, and sparking dialogue about ethical issues. They allow us to step into the shoes of others, to see the world through different lenses, and to grapple with the complexities of human experience.

One of the primary roles of arts and culture is to foster ethical expression. Through storytelling, music, and visual representations, artists and creators can explore ethical dilemmas, challenge societal injustices, and inspire action for positive change. They can give voice to marginalized groups, raise awareness of social issues, and spark conversations that lead to greater understanding and empathy.

Literature, for instance, can transport us to different times and places, exposing us to diverse perspectives and challenging our assumptions about the world. By reading stories about characters from different backgrounds and facing different challenges, we can develop a deeper understanding of the human condition and cultivate empathy for those who are different from us.

Music, with its universal language, can evoke a wide range of emotions and connect people across cultures. Through music, we can experience joy, sorrow, anger, and hope, and we can find solace and inspiration in the face of adversity. Music can also be a powerful tool for social activism, as musicians use their platform to raise awareness of social issues and advocate for change.

Visual arts, such as painting, sculpture, and photography, can capture the beauty and complexity of the world around us. They can also challenge our perceptions, provoke thought, and inspire action. Visual artists can use their work to comment on social issues, to document historical events, and to create spaces for dialogue and reflection.

Theater and dance provide a platform for exploring human relationships, emotions, and social dynamics. Through performance, we can witness the struggles and triumphs of others, and we can gain a deeper understanding of the complexities of human behavior. Theater and dance can also be used to challenge stereotypes, to promote social justice, and to inspire collective action.

Film, as a powerful medium of storytelling, has the ability to reach a vast audience and to shape public opinion. Films can raise awareness of social issues, challenge stereotypes, and inspire empathy for marginalized groups. They can also spark conversations about ethical dilemmas and encourage viewers to reflect on their own values and beliefs.

In addition to fostering ethical expression, arts and culture also play a crucial role in nurturing critical thinking skills. By engaging with art and cultural works, we are challenged to interpret, analyze, and evaluate different perspectives and interpretations. This process of critical inquiry can help us to develop a more nuanced understanding of complex issues and to make more informed decisions about our own lives and the world around us.

Moreover, arts and culture can inspire empathy and compassion. By immersing ourselves in the stories, music, and images created by others, we can gain a deeper understanding of their experiences, their struggles, and their joys. This can lead to a greater sense of connection and empathy, breaking down barriers of prejudice and fostering a more inclusive society.

The role of arts and culture in nurturing ethical expression is not limited to formal settings such as museums and theaters. It can also be found in everyday life, in the music we listen to, the books we read, and the films we watch. By engaging with arts and culture in all its forms, we can cultivate a more ethical and compassionate world.

In conclusion, arts and culture play a vital role in nurturing ethical expression, fostering critical thinking, and inspiring empathy and compassion. By recognizing and harnessing the power of arts and culture, we can create a more just, equitable, and harmonious society.

❧❧❧

Ethics is not just about following rules; it's about making choices that align with our values and contribute to the greater good. Let us empower our students to become ethical decision-makers who can navigate the complexities of the modern world with integrity and compassion. Remember, our choices define who we are and the kind of world we create.

EIGHTEEN

ASSESSMENT AND EVALUATION: MEASURING ETHICAL GROWTH

Assessment and evaluation play a crucial role in any educational endeavor. However, when the focus shifts to ethical growth, traditional methods of measurement often fall short. Ethical growth, unlike academic achievement, is not easily quantifiable through standardized tests or grades. It involves a complex interplay of values, beliefs, and behaviors that evolve over time.

Therefore, assessing and evaluating ethical growth requires a more nuanced and holistic approach, one that takes into account the multifaceted nature of ethical development.

Traditionally, education systems have focused on assessing cognitive skills and knowledge acquisition through standardized tests, quizzes, and exams. While these methods are useful for measuring academic proficiency, they do not adequately capture the intricacies of ethical growth.

Ethical development is not a linear process; it involves grappling with complex moral dilemmas, navigating conflicting values, and making decisions in real-world contexts.

To effectively measure ethical growth, we need to move beyond traditional assessment methods and embrace a more comprehensive approach. This involves assessing not only what students know about ethics but also how they apply that knowledge in their lives. It involves evaluating their ability to reason morally, to empathize with others, and to make ethical decisions in complex situations.

One way to assess ethical growth is through self-reflection and self-assessment. By encouraging students to reflect on their own values, beliefs, and behaviors, we can gain valuable insights into their ethical development.

This can be done through journaling, discussions, or structured self-assessment tools. By engaging in self-reflection, students can become more aware of their own ethical strengths and weaknesses, and they can identify areas where they need to grow.

Another approach is to use peer assessment. This involves asking students to evaluate each other's ethical behavior and decision-making. By providing feedback to their peers, students can gain a deeper understanding of ethical principles and learn from each other's experiences. Peer assessment can also foster a sense of accountability and encourage students to take responsibility for their own ethical development.

In addition to self-assessment and peer assessment, teachers can also assess ethical growth through observation and anecdotal records. By observing students in various settings, such as the classroom, extracurricular activities, and community service projects, teachers can gain a holistic understanding of their ethical behavior and decision-making.

Anecdotal records, which document specific instances of ethical behavior or growth, can provide valuable evidence of student progress over time.

Portfolios can also be a useful tool for assessing ethical growth. By collecting and curating artifacts of their ethical development, such as reflections, essays, and projects, students can create a tangible record of their progress. Portfolios can also be used to showcase student work to parents, teachers, and potential employers, demonstrating their commitment to ethical values and social responsibility.

In addition to these formative assessment methods, summative assessments can also be used to evaluate ethical growth at the end of a course or program. These assessments can take various forms, such as essays, presentations, or simulations.

They should be designed to assess students' ability to apply ethical principles to real-world scenarios and to make informed and reasoned decisions.

The assessment of ethical growth should not be limited to the classroom. It should also extend into the community, where students can demonstrate their ethical values through service learning projects, volunteer work, and other forms of civic engagement.

By assessing their impact on the community, we can gain a more comprehensive understanding of their ethical development.

In conclusion, assessing and evaluating ethical growth is a complex and multifaceted endeavor. It requires a shift from traditional assessment methods that focus on knowledge acquisition to a more holistic approach that takes into account the complexity of ethical development.

By incorporating self-reflection, peer assessment, observation, anecdotal records, portfolios, and summative assessments, we can gain a deeper understanding of how students are growing ethically and provide them with the feedback and support they need to continue their journey towards ethical maturity.

ϷϷϷ

The most important lessons are not found in textbooks, but in the hearts and minds of those around us. Let us create a learning environment where students learn from each other, from their teachers, and from the community at large. Remember, education is a collaborative endeavor that requires the engagement of all stakeholders.

NINETEEN

POLICY AND PRACTICE: REFORMING JAPAN'S EDUCATION SYSTEM

Japan's education system has long been lauded for its rigor, discipline, and high academic standards. However, in recent decades, concerns have arisen regarding its ability to adapt to the changing needs of the 21st century. The system has been criticized for its emphasis on rote memorization, standardized testing, and conformity, which can stifle creativity, critical thinking, and individual expression. Recognizing the need for reform, policymakers and educators in Japan have embarked on a journey to reimagine the education system, seeking to strike a balance between academic excellence and holistic development.

One of the key areas of reform is the move towards a more student-centered approach to learning. This involves shifting away from teacher-centered lectures and rote learning towards active learning methods that encourage student participation, collaboration, and critical thinking. Project-based learning, inquiry-based learning, and flipped classrooms are some of the approaches being adopted to foster a more engaging and relevant learning experience.

Another area of reform is the emphasis on developing 21st-century skills, such as critical thinking, creativity, communication, and collaboration. These skills are essential for success in the modern workplace and for navigating the complexities of an increasingly interconnected world. To foster these skills, schools are introducing new subjects, such as coding and entrepreneurship, and integrating technology into the classroom.

The Japanese government has also recognized the importance of global competence in preparing students for the globalized world. This involves developing cross-cultural understanding, language proficiency, and the ability to collaborate with people from different backgrounds. Schools are increasingly offering international exchange programs, language immersion courses, and opportunities for students to engage with global issues.

In addition to these curricular reforms, there is also a growing emphasis on the holistic development of students. This involves addressing their social, emotional, and physical well-being, as well as their academic needs. Schools are introducing programs to promote mental health, mindfulness, and physical activity, recognizing that these factors are essential for overall well-being and academic success.

Reforming Japan's education system is not without its challenges. One of the main obstacles is the deeply ingrained culture of academic pressure and competition. Parents often place a high value on academic achievement and expect their children to excel in school. This pressure can lead to stress, anxiety, and even mental health problems in students. To address this issue, policymakers and educators are working to create a more supportive and inclusive learning environment, where students feel valued and encouraged to pursue their passions.

Another challenge is the resistance to change from some educators and administrators who are accustomed to traditional teaching methods and assessment practices. Implementing new pedagogical approaches and curriculum reforms requires significant training and support for teachers. The government is investing in professional development programs for teachers and providing resources to schools to help them adapt to the changing landscape of education.

The COVID-19 pandemic has also had a significant impact on Japan's education system, accelerating the adoption of online learning and digital technologies. While this has presented challenges, it has also created opportunities to rethink the way education is delivered and to make it more accessible and flexible for students.

In conclusion, reforming Japan's education system is a complex and ongoing process. It involves addressing a wide range of issues, from curriculum reform and pedagogical innovation to student well-being and teacher training. However, the commitment to creating a more student-centered, holistic, and globally competent education system is evident. By embracing change and fostering innovation, Japan is paving the way for a brighter future for its students and for the country as a whole.

❦❦❦

The true measure of a school's success is not just its academic achievements, but the kind of citizens it produces. Let us strive to create schools that graduate students who are not only knowledgeable but also compassionate, ethical, and committed to making a positive impact on the world. Remember, the future of our society depends on the values we instill in our children.

TWENTY

A Vision for the Future: Envisioning Ethical Schools

Envisioning a future where ethical schools are the norm is not just a utopian dream, but a necessary aspiration in our ever-evolving society. Ethical schools are more than just institutions that impart knowledge; they are communities that nurture values, character, and a sense of social responsibility. They are places where students learn to think critically, act compassionately, and strive for a more just and equitable world. By fostering a culture of ethics and values, these schools can empower students to become responsible citizens, ethical leaders, and agents of positive change.

At the heart of an ethical school lies a strong moral compass. This compass is not dictated by a single set of rules or doctrines, but rather emerges from a collective commitment to certain core values. These values may include honesty, integrity, respect, compassion, fairness, and social responsibility. By embedding these values into every aspect of school life, from curriculum design to classroom interactions to extracurricular activities, ethical schools create an environment where students are constantly exposed to and encouraged to practice these values.

Ethical schools recognize that learning is not just about acquiring knowledge and skills, but also about developing character and moral reasoning. They prioritize the teaching of ethics alongside traditional academic subjects, ensuring that students are equipped with the tools to navigate complex moral dilemmas and make informed decisions. This involves creating opportunities for students to engage in discussions about ethical issues, to reflect on their own values and beliefs, and to practice ethical decision-making in real-world scenarios.

An ethical school is also a community that values diversity and inclusion. It recognizes that students come from different backgrounds, have different experiences, and hold different beliefs. By embracing this diversity, ethical schools create a rich tapestry of perspectives and experiences that enriches the learning environment for everyone. They foster a culture of respect and understanding, where students learn to appreciate differences and to work collaboratively with others who may not share their views.

In an ethical school, teachers are not just instructors, but also mentors and role models. They embody the values that the school seeks to instill in its students, and they create a classroom environment that is safe, supportive, and conducive to ethical exploration. Teachers encourage students to question, to challenge, and to think for themselves. They help students to develop their own moral compasses and to become critical thinkers who can engage with complex ethical issues.

Beyond the classroom, an ethical school extends its reach into the community. It partners with local organizations, businesses, and government agencies to create opportunities for students to engage in service learning projects and to make a positive impact on their communities. This not only reinforces the values of social responsibility and civic engagement, but also provides students with real-world experience and a deeper understanding of the challenges facing their communities.

The vision of ethical schools is not without its challenges. In a world that often prioritizes individual achievement and material success, fostering a culture of ethics and values can be an uphill battle. There may be resistance from parents who prioritize academic achievement over character development, from teachers who are not trained in ethical pedagogy, and from policymakers who focus on standardized testing and accountability measures.

However, the benefits of ethical schools are undeniable. Students who attend ethical schools are more likely to exhibit prosocial behavior, to engage in civic activities, and to make ethical choices in their personal and professional lives. They are better equipped to navigate the complexities of the modern world, to build strong relationships, and to contribute to a more just and equitable society.

The vision of ethical schools is not just a dream, but a necessity. In a world that is increasingly interconnected and interdependent, the ability to think ethically and to act with compassion and integrity is more important than ever. By investing in ethical schools, we are investing in the future of our children, our communities, and our planet.

ᗡᗡᗡ

The legacy of ethical education is not measured in test scores or awards, but in the lives it transforms and the positive change it inspires. Let us commit ourselves to creating a legacy of ethical education that will shape a brighter future for generations to come. Remember, education is not just about preparing for the future; it's about creating it.

TWENTY-ONE
SUMMARY

Ethics and Value-Based Education: A Blueprint for Reimagining Japan's School System

In a rapidly changing world marked by technological advancements, globalization, and complex social challenges, the need for a comprehensive and holistic approach to education has never been more apparent. This book, "Ethics and Value-Based Education: Reimagining Japan's School System," delves into the critical need for a paradigm shift in Japanese education, moving beyond the traditional emphasis on academic achievement to cultivate well-rounded individuals equipped with strong ethical values, critical thinking skills, and a deep sense of social responsibility.

The book begins by exploring the heart of ethical education, emphasizing that it transcends mere academics. Ethical education seeks to instill moral reasoning, empathy, and a sense of responsibility towards oneself and others. It prepares students to navigate complex ethical dilemmas, make informed decisions, and contribute to the common good in an interconnected world. In Japan, where academic rigor and discipline have long been prioritized, there is a growing recognition of the need to nurture ethical values alongside academic pursuits. This involves creating a supportive and inclusive learning environment, incorporating ethical discussions into the curriculum, and providing opportunities for students to practice ethical decision-making and social responsibility.

The importance of values in the classroom is highlighted as more than just words on a blackboard. Values such as honesty, respect, responsibility, compassion, and fairness provide a moral compass that guides individuals in making sound decisions and building healthy relationships. In Japan, the concept of "tokubetsu katsudo," or special activities, emphasizes character development and social skills, but challenges such as the pressure to succeed in entrance exams and the changing landscape of traditional values need to be addressed through innovative approaches like experiential learning and technology integration.

A new curriculum is proposed, one that teaches character alongside knowledge. This involves rethinking what and how we teach, incorporating character education into every aspect of the learning experience. Teachers become facilitators, guiding students to explore their values, beliefs, and identities. Experiential learning through service projects, internships, and community engagement initiatives provide students with opportunities to apply their knowledge and skills in real-world contexts, fostering social responsibility and a deeper understanding of the world. Assessment methods shift to focus on measuring growth in character traits, such as empathy, resilience, and leadership, using tools like self-reflection journals, peer feedback, and portfolios.

The book emphasizes the shift from competition to collaboration, reimagining school culture to be less about individual achievement and more about teamwork, cooperation, and mutual support. Collaborative learning environments have been shown to improve academic achievement, self-esteem, and social skills, while fostering a more positive and inclusive school climate. This shift requires rethinking the role of teachers as facilitators, redesigning physical spaces for group work, and leveraging technology to enable collaboration.

Preparing students for real-world challenges involves addressing moral dilemmas, situations where values clash and there are no easy answers. By presenting students with hypothetical scenarios and real-world examples, educators can help them develop critical thinking skills, analyze different perspectives, and cultivate empathy and compassion. Teaching ethical decision-making equips students to navigate the complexities of the real world and make informed and ethical choices.

The role of teachers in guiding ethical development is paramount. As role models, mentors, and facilitators, teachers create a safe and inclusive learning environment, provide opportunities for ethical decision-making practice, and integrate ethical considerations into the curriculum. Teachers also play a vital role in shaping school culture by promoting respect, inclusivity, and social responsibility.

Parents are recognized as essential partners in supporting values education at home and school. By modeling values, actively teaching ethics and morality, building strong relationships with teachers, and creating opportunities for ethical decision-making practice outside of school, parents can reinforce the values taught in the classroom and contribute to their children's holistic development.

Community connections offer valuable learning experiences beyond the classroom walls. By engaging with their communities through volunteering, participating in events, and interacting with diverse individuals, students develop social responsibility, gain practical skills, and broaden their understanding of the world. These connections also benefit communities by tapping into the energy and fresh perspectives of young people.

Global citizenship is emphasized as a crucial framework for understanding our role and responsibilities in an interconnected world. It calls upon us to act with empathy, compassion, and a sense of shared responsibility towards each other and the planet. Ethics is central to global citizenship, guiding our actions and decisions. Education plays a vital role in fostering global citizenship by teaching students about different cultures, perspectives, and global issues, and encouraging them to think critically and take action to make a positive difference.

The book also delves into the ethical implications of technology in the digital age. It highlights the need for responsible information consumption, ethical use of social media, fair and transparent AI development, protection of worker rights in the gig economy, safeguarding privacy, and respecting intellectual property. Education, policymaking, and individual responsibility are key to navigating these ethical challenges.

Environmental responsibility is another critical aspect explored, emphasizing the need for education to foster a deep understanding of our interconnectedness with the natural world and a sense of stewardship for the planet. Environmental education raises awareness of environmental issues, builds knowledge and understanding, fosters critical thinking, and instills values such as respect for nature and a commitment to sustainability.

Valuing all voices and promoting diversity and inclusion are essential for creating a just and equitable society. By recognizing the unique contributions that each individual brings to the table, fostering a sense of belonging, and celebrating diversity, we can build stronger communities, create more innovative workplaces, and empower students to become responsible and engaged citizens.

Social justice is highlighted as a crucial component of education.

By raising awareness of systemic inequalities, fostering critical consciousness, and teaching advocacy skills, educators can empower students to challenge injustice, advocate for marginalized groups, and create a more equitable world. This empowerment not only benefits individuals and communities but is also essential for addressing global challenges.

The book concludes by envisioning ethical schools as communities that nurture values, character, and a sense of social responsibility. These schools prioritize ethical education alongside academic subjects, embrace diversity and inclusion, and foster a culture of respect and understanding. While challenges exist in creating such schools, the benefits are undeniable, leading to students who are not only academically successful but also compassionate, ethical, and engaged citizens ready to make a positive impact on the world.

❦❦❦

Citation And References

This book represents the culmination of extensive research and meticulous analysis, incorporating a diverse range of sources, including numerous books, scholarly studies, and personal experiences. Additionally, I have scoured various websites to gather relevant information and data essential for the compilation of this work. I have taken every precaution to ensure the accuracy of the information presented and have diligently cited all sources to acknowledge their contributions.

Despite these efforts, the possibility of inadvertent errors remains. I deeply value the insights of my readers and appreciate any feedback that can help identify and rectify such inaccuracies. I encourage you to bring any discrepancies to my attention.

Your feedback is not only welcome but crucial, as it will aid in correcting current editions and enhancing the content of future ones. I am committed to maintaining the highest standards of accuracy and reliability in my work and thank you for your support and understanding.

Additionally, I firmly uphold the principle of freedom of speech and expression as guaranteed under Article 19(1)(a) of the Constitution of India, and I respect the diverse viewpoints and expressions of all readers.

ϼϼϼ

Other Books Of The Author

1. Empowering Minds: A Journey into Women's Self-Discovery and Power
2. The Dynamics of Motivation: Catalyzing Thought into Action
3. Meditation and Mental Well Being: The Path to Inner Peace and Clarity
4. The Psychology of Child Education: Nurturing Future Generations
5. Ethical Enlightenment: A Modern Guide to Living with Integrity
6. Voices of Empowerment: Stories of Women Rising Against Odds
7. Social Psychology in Everyday Life: Understanding Human Connections
8. The Essence of Motivational Speaking: Inspiring Change in Others
9. Balancing Acts: Women, Work, and the Will to Lead
10. Guiding with Grace: Raising Children with Compassion and Awareness
11. The Power of Positive Aging: Embracing Life After Fifty
12. Building Resilient Communities: Social Work in Action
13. The Ethical Educator: Principles for Teaching and Learning
14. From Insight to Impact: Social Psychology for a Better World
15. The Ethics of Empathy: A Guide to Ethical Living
16. The Science of Empowering the Self: Navigating Life's Challenges with Psychological Wisdom
17. The Mindful Conscious Leader: Meditation Techniques for Modern Management
18. Pioneering Spirit: Women's Pathways to Leadership and Empowerment
19. Feeling to Healing: The Role of Emotional Intelligence in Child Development
20. Transformative Talks and Words of Inspiration: Insights into Motivational Oratory

Bhajan
101. Pilgrimage of the Soul: Spiritual Journeys in India

ঢ়ঢ়ঢ়

• 133 •

Contact

Dr. Minakshi Bansal
Social Activist
Ahmedabad, Gujarat, Bharat
minakshiindiag20@yahoo.com

❧❧❧

|| LOKAHA SAMASTHAHA SUKHINO BHAVANTU ||